Woof!

ISBN: 978-1-64030-386-7

YOU HAD ME AT woof

new seasons®

Wanna go outside? Let's go outside. Can we go outside? We should go outside. Have you been outside?

I know I messed up, but people really need to realize they can't have nice things and a puppy.

I may not be able to run anymore, but I'm wise enough to appreciate the days when I could.

I wasn't lost, you were.

I ran. I got the ball.
I brought it back.
Now what?

You should see the other guy.

You want me to apologize
to the cat...really?

So many choices, so little time....

What cookie? I didn't hide a cookie. I don't know what you're talking about....

Sorry, I think I was sick the day they covered not doing this in obedience school.

Maybe this will make up
for what I did in the garden.

At least I didn't get my paw
caught in the cookie jar....

I'm not lying about that missing turkey leg.... What do you mean my nose is growing?

Hair on the couch? Not mine....

Well, you put a slipcover on it,
so we thought it was ours now.

What smell?

I overheard you saying
your moisturizer helps with
age spots...so I ate it.

I know. I have the
right to remain silent.

Please don't send me
back to obedience school!

What does the fox say NOW?

What happens in Vegas...
stays in Vegas!

Where did you come from,
intriguing object? Don't worry,
I'll keep an eye on you.

You look familiar.

Bow. Wow.

Mmmm! Yes!

A vintage classic—circa 1974.

I detect a hint of wet wool

with overtones of argyle.

Triple threat!

I can't possibly go
anywhere in this outfit.

How many dogs does it take to change a roll of toilet paper? Yeah, I've heard that one before.

Could be food...could be not food.

What?

One more step and these pants are mine!

Do I smell ham?

When was there ham?

I've never found a puppy I didn't like.

I'm not pouting!

Nope. Not a dog.

I hereby claim this pot to be my
hiding place for most of your stuff.

Really? A sweater?
It's 100 degrees outside, lady.

You had me at woof.

This cardboard box
just isn't my scene.

You do not own a dog, the dog owns you.

—Unknown

Psst...

The humans are watching.

Go inside?
I think not.

I heard you the first time!
I won't do it again.

Is that a box of tissues
left unattended?
JACKPOT!

Uh, you guys might want to sleep downstairs tonight.

I hate going for walks,
but without me, the ladies
just ignore him.

I plead the Fifth.

I swear I wore my
retainer every night!

There'd better be a prize at
the bottom of all this!

Maybe if I
chew this up
enough they'll
get rid of it.

Are you in a "time-out"?

Now you'll have to
take me with you...
I ate the keys.

With special thanks to:
Jack Alexander, Jennifer Barney, Cary Cochrane, Kate Cochrane, Lisa Cochrane, Karen Hartman, Christopher Hiltz, Michael G. Ibrahim, Anne O'Connor, Maggie O'Connor, Frank Putrino, Anita Remijas, Barbara Rittenhouse, Mimi Roeder, Kathleen Rose, Ingrid Serio, Helene Shapiro, Patty Sprague, Linda Weber, Leslie Weyhrich